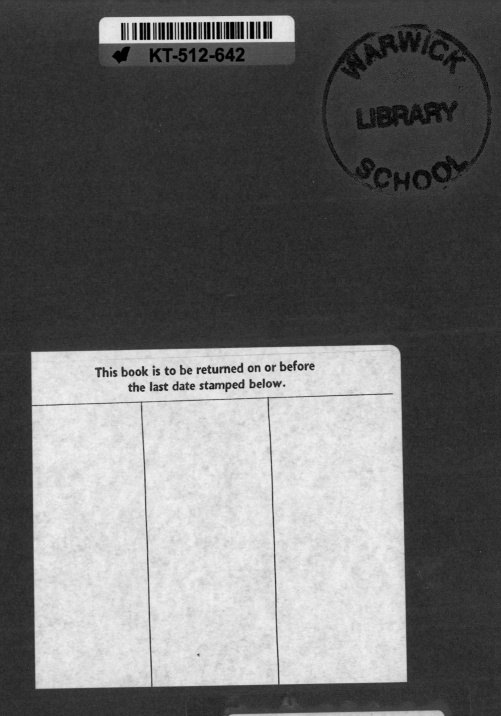

TALKING ABOUT MYSELF

RELATIONSHIPS & SEX

Interviews by Angela Neustatter
Photographs by Laurence Cendrowicz

W

FRANKLIN WATTS
LONDON • SYDNEY

First published in 2008 by Franklin Watts

Franklin Watts,
338 Euston Road,
London, NW1 3BH

Franklin Watts Australia,
Level 17/207 Kent Street,
Sydney, NSW 2000

Series editor: Sarah Peutrill
Art Director: Jonathan Hair
Design: Elaine Wilkinson
Panels written by: Sarah Ridley
Researcher: Charlotte Wormald
Photographs: Laurence Cendrowicz (unless otherwise stated)

The Author and Publisher would like to thank the
interviewees for their contributions to this book.
Also thanks to Anita Bennett.

Picture credits: Olly Hoeben: 14. Ad Doward/iStockphoto: 11
Joseph/Shutterstock: 8. jkita/Shutterstock: 9. MalibuBooks: 6.
Stefan Redel/Shutterstock 20. Roman Sigaev/Shutterstock: 5.

Dewey number: 306.7

ISBN: 978 0 7496 7707 7

Printed in China

Franklin Watts is a division of Hachette Children's Books,
an Hachette Livre UK company.

CONTENTS

FIRST RELATIONSHIPS

Puberty is the time when sexual maturity begins and along with it there may be powerful attractions and erotic feelings. Many people experience their first relationship in their teens. A relationship may involve only hand holding and kissing. For others, one or both may want sex to be part of the relationship, particularly when trust and affection develop.

Understanding your sexuality

For the majority of people, a sexual relationship means one between a man and a woman. Heterosexuality is the norm and society favours this. However, a small number of us find that we are attracted to people of our own sex, some people find both men and women sexually attractive, and some choose not to be sexual at all. The teenage years are the time when we discover 'who we are'.

Under pressure

Deciding whether to have sex or not can be difficult. We live in a highly sexualised culture and the media

carries a lot of material making us believe we should look and act sexy. And there may be peer pressure to have sex, often before you really want to. A survey found that close to half of 3,000 students aged 15–18 were involved in sex where one partner was not equally willing. It also found that almost three in ten girls lost their virginity for 'negative reasons' such as wanting to please a boyfriend, and two in five of the young people wished they had waited longer before having sex.

The first time

It is important to wait until you really feel ready. You should never be bullied into having sex by someone telling you other people do it. It is interesting that James, who tells how he sleeps around (page 8), actually likes girls who, 'don't give up their bodies easily' more than those who quickly sleep with him. Losing your virginity is an important step and you may feel upset afterwards if it happens on a casual one-night stand or with someone you really don't care about. Drink can be one reason this happens. An alarming number of young people end up having sex because they are drunk. If you find it hard to talk about sex with your partner then you are not ready. There is no rush – indeed some people believe that you should wait for marriage before you have sex.

Safe sex

If you are old enough (in Britain the legal age you may have sex is 16, and males who sleep with girls younger than this risk prosecution whatever their age) and happy to have sex then it is essential you protect yourself and your partner. Sexually transmitted infections (STIs) are on the increase and Britain has the highest rate of unplanned teenage pregnancy in Europe. Myths such as 'you cannot get pregnant the first time' are untrue and dangerous. See page 23 for more myths about sex.

Relationship breakdown

Teenage relationships often do not last, but may be part of how we learn about relating to someone else as a partner. When a relationship breaks down it can be painful and if you are very upset it is worth talking to supportive friends and parents, or a school counsellor. Otherwise contact one of the helplines or organisations for young people on page 31.

Sexual abuse

Ami describes in her interview the shocking sexual abuse she endured as a child (page 26). Like too many other children she was too frightened to tell and it seriously damaged her ability to make happy relationships and enjoy sex. Sexual abuse can happen to boys or girls and it is most often carried out by someone known to the child. If it is happening to you do tell someone. Ringing Childline (see page 31) is a good first step and they will guide you as to what to do next. It is very important to understand that you have not done anything wrong – forcing anyone to have sex or perform a sexual act is illegal.

SAFER SEX

Safer sex isn't just about preventing pregnancy but is also about avoiding sexually transmitted infections (STIs). The more sexual partners you have, the higher your risk of catching an infection. However, some people are unlucky and will catch something from the only person they have ever slept with. There has been a rise in the number of people affected by sexually transmitted infections in recent years.

WEAR A CONDOM

The surest way to have safer sex is to use a condom. The condom protects both partners from catching STIs, as well as preventing pregnancy. GP surgeries and some NHS clinics give out free condoms and you can buy them from shops, supermarkets and chemists.

HIDDEN DANGER

It is often impossible to tell that someone has a sexually transmitted infection. If you notice changes in your body or become anxious about possible exposure to disease after unprotected sex, consult your doctor or a family planning clinic for advice. If you know you are carrying a sexually transmitted infection, the right thing to do is to be honest and take the necessary precautions to prevent it from spreading to someone else.

TREATMENT

Some diseases, like Chlamydia, gonorrhoea and syphilis, can be treated and cured with antibiotics. Left untreated, however, they can cause future health problems and infertility. Other diseases, including hepatitis B, genital herpes and HIV, cannot be cured and have to be managed over the lifetime of the affected person.

SLEEPING AROUND

Janine tried to prove to herself that she was attractive by sleeping around. It made her very unhappy, but she is now learning to like herself.

Photo posed by model.

I lost my virginity when I was 17 and I was happy about it. I wasn't actually going out with the guy, but he was a good friend who was also a virgin and it was very sweet and gentle. I was happy to leave it at that and I didn't sleep with anyone else for a while. But I was very unhappy when my parents separated and my dad wasn't around much. I felt very lost. I went on a gap year with a group who all put a huge emphasis on personal looks. I was seeking approval and because it seemed to come with sex I slept with a lot of people.

One-night stands

When I came back I was really skint and miserable. I started drinking a lot and having one-night stands. I just wanted proof that I was attractive. However casual sex doesn't do anything for self-esteem and there were horrific mornings waking up with a stranger who didn't want you there. But I got into the mindset of proving I could sleep with anyone I wanted. That's the message some women's magazines promote, that being predatory is being an empowered 21st-century woman.

Sometimes I slept with longstanding male friends and we might have sex more than once, but it was never going to turn into a proper relationship. My behaviour became a habit. It got to the point that when I went out my mission would be to have sex with somebody – it didn't really matter who. I would get horrifically drunk and go after someone.

Taking a STI test

I worried a lot about getting a STI. I was really scared waiting for the results of a STI test. Sometimes I insisted on condoms but not always and I think that is typical. Even now I still have to go for another test.

A new start

I met my boyfriend when I was 21. I slept with him the first time we met and thought that would be that, but he got my number and called. I was still in my pattern of behaviour and during the first six months with him I slept with other people. I did it when I didn't feel happy with the relationship. But I wanted it to work and I decided I needed to cut all the male friends I had slept with out of my life.

Liking myself

I realised I could change. I gave up drink and I began to see I could enjoy meeting new people and not sleep with someone. I began to make new friends and to start liking myself better. I am studying again and that feels good. I feel confident that if I split up with my boyfriend now the last thing I will focus on is sex. I've found out the hard way that you can't make yourself better through others. ∎

"I gave up drink and I began to see I could enjoy meeting new people and not sleep with someone."

SELF-ESTEEM AND SEX

Our self-esteem is the way we feel about ourselves. If we have high self-esteem we like ourselves, feel happy with the way we are and confident in our abilities. If we compare ourselves badly against others and don't like ourselves and feel unhappy with our appearance or abilities we have low self-esteem.

RISK-TAKING

Someone with low self-esteem is more likely to take sexual risks. They may confuse sex with love or feel that having sex will make them appear more cool. They may even fear that the boy/girl who wants sex with them will tell other people that they are frigid if they refuse. Without the confidence to say 'no', some people end up sleeping with people that they don't really like.

STEP BACK

If you are feeling unsure about having sex with someone try to take a step back. Make an excuse about needing to go home or feeling ill. Then you will have time to think.

BUILDING SELF-ESTEEM

Changing self-esteem can take time. Sometimes it helps to talk to family, friends or a counsellor. People can help themselves by focusing on the positive rather than being too self-critical. Several websites have useful tips on how to build self-esteem (see page 31).

SEX WITHOUT ATTACHMENT

James enjoys having sex with lots of different girls but doesn't want attachment.

Photos posed by models.

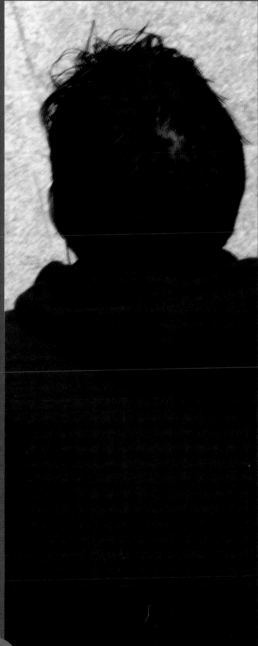

I have a brother four years older and he had porn magazines around. Through these I began to be interested in girls and sexuality when I was at puberty. I was small for my age and girls would talk about me as 'sweet' and I assumed a cocky cheekiness, responding to this, I think out of shyness, but it gave me confidence.

First experiences

I began going out with girls from about 13, doing everything but having actual sex. There was a lot of sexual chemistry going on – girls in short skirts... alcohol... everything amazing and new, but it's also scary in a way. I enjoyed experimenting but I didn't really feel in a hurry as some of my friends were.

In fact I lost my virginity quite late – I was 17 and I lost it with a girl who was seven years older than me when I was in Brazil on my 'liberation tour!' – my gap year. I really enjoyed it and knew I wanted more.

"I enjoyed experimenting but I didn't really feel in a hurry as some of my friends were."

Anonymous sex

The attraction of getting together with a girl can be different: last time it happened it was with a girl I really didn't fancy at all but it was late at night and sex was available and I thought, 'Why not?' Or I might pursue a girl because she just turns me on although I've hardly met her. I meet girls in pubs, at parties. It's really exciting having sex with someone you don't know.

I haven't had any long-term relationships – three months seems an age when you are young. The longest I have had is a few months. I get itchy feet very easily. I have met girls who I imagine I might have liked a relationship with but they haven't been interested. And I do think guys naturally want to have sex with a lot of girls. Even when you are really happy going out with a girl you see someone else and think, 'I would like to sleep with her'.

"I don't respect girls who sleep with me easily. I know it's a terrible thing to say when I behave the way I do ..."

Double standards

I don't respect girls who sleep with me easily. I know it's a terrible thing to say when I behave the way I do, but it's the truth. I tell my sister don't sleep with a guy

on the first date. As guys we are more attracted to girls who don't give up their bodies easily. On the other hand I can see a girl might just want to have sex, as I do, and why shouldn't she? It's not logical or fair.

There have been girls who have got upset because I've moved on after sleeping with them a couple of times, but I don't feel bad. I don't lead girls on.

Safe sex

I have worried about STIs so I have tried to be as safe as possible and I haven't ever caught one - yet. I think it's a big issue and I'm surprised how many girls, once you are in the mood, would not object to unprotected sex. Yet all the advertising regarding safe sex seems to be geared towards young men.

My future

I think if you have a past where you've slept with different girls it might mean you've got something out of your system. There is a part of me that thinks one day I will settle down but for now I just want to have fun; I want to learn as much about as many people as I can. Perhaps it's self-protection not wanting to get attached. ∎

GLAD TO BE GAY

Shari, 15, realised she was gay aged 11 and she thanks her parents for helping her feel good about herself.

I never wanted to wear dresses or be like a girl. And when I was 11 I told my mother I wanted a sex change so I could have a girlfriend. She said that was a bit drastic but perhaps I was trying to tell her I was gay, and we would see. She was cool and that was really good, although I know she has cried sometimes worrying about the problems I might have. My parents are separated but my dad was fine with it as well – his line is he likes women too!

Outsider

I was at an all-girls school and I felt an outsider when they all brought in make-up and hair stuff, worrying about how they looked. I felt very lonely so I went on the Internet and found gay chatrooms and that became my social world. I met my first girlfriend who was a sexual partner this way. It felt so right and normal I wondered why every girl wasn't into this.

"I felt very lonely so I went on the Internet and found gay chatrooms and that became my social world."

HOMOSEXUALITY

Homosexuals are attracted to people of the same sex. It describes men who fancy men and women who fancy women. Homosexual men are often described as gay, while homosexual women are called gay or lesbian.

TEENAGE CONFUSION

As young people grow up, their sexuality develops. Many teenagers experience strong feelings for people of both sexes at different times. Some people develop a 'crush' on someone of the same sex as themselves, whether it be a teacher or a friend. It can all be very confusing. However, if someone is attracted to people of the same sex over a long period of time, they are likely to be homosexual. It is estimated that about one in ten people is homosexual.

BISEXUALS

Bisexuals are attracted to people of both sexes at different times in their lives, or at the same time.

That didn't last but the next relationship from the net lasted for eight fantastic months. People ask me why I don't try going out with boys to see if I might like that, as though I might discover I'd got things wrong, but I have no interest whatsoever.

Happy in my own skin

People say I am young to be so sure about my sexuality but I have no confusion about it. I enjoy gay sex; I love my androgynous dress style and spiky hair and the fact that gay women look at me on the street. I also love it that girlfriends feel they can come out to me because I will understand. One was able to come out to her whole family after we had spoken about how she might do so.

I think if my close girlfriends who are straight didn't accept me, or refused to let me discuss my relationships, it would be much harder to feel so okay about myself. And I do see the difficulties some of my peers have knowing they are expected to grow up and have families with children. There's one boy who doesn't dare come out to his dad, and the mother of a friend said, when she came out, 'Oh what you need is a hunky rugby player.'

In future

I might like to have a child sometime and although I wouldn't expect to have it naturally I would want a male role model in its life. Someone the kid could call Dad – I think that is important. My dad is important in my life.

I wish everyone gay could be as lucky as I have been in being accepted. It is the difference between being confident and feeling as good as anyone else, and constantly trying to disguise yourself. I would say to parents the most loving thing they can do is be really supportive of their gay child. ∎

DEALING WITH HOMOPHOBIA

Joe realised he was gay while at an all-boys school. He suffered homophobic abuse and ran away to live on the streets of London.

Q When were you aware of being gay?

As a young child I chose to play with girls and I sensed there was something different about me. My parents had friends who were gay, so I told my mother. She advised me to wait a while and not rush into deciding who and what I was.

Q Was that helpful?

I felt my parents were on my side so when I was about 14 and having sexual feelings about boys I needed my parents to understand. They had suspected it and were absolutely supportive, so I didn't have the really difficult situation some gay young people do where their families are very shocked or reject them.

Q Did that make it easy to come out to others?

I didn't choose to do it. It happened because I was standing up for a young boy who was being picked on and called gay. I said, 'Well so what if he is? It's got nothing to do with you.'

> *"Immediately the story went around that I was gay. There was a lot of verbal abuse. People called me 'queer boy' and said, 'Don't come near me.'"*

 ## What was the result of doing this?

Immediately the story went around that I was gay. There was a lot of verbal abuse. People called me 'queer boy' and said, 'Don't come near me.' A chant went around, 'Put your bums on the ground when Joe's around.' I felt I wasn't human in their eyes. It made me very unhappy and very angry.

 ## Did you have friends you could talk to?

I told a few close friends but then one told about me publicly and I felt dreadfully betrayed. I decided I must deal with being gay alone. Even though the school was tough on racism and Section 28 (see page 15) had been repealed, they did nothing about homophobia.

 ## Did you talk to your parents?

I didn't because my school had a culture of being a man and dealing with things on your own. It would have been much better to tell. ▶

> *"I felt I wasn't human in their eyes. It made me very unhappy and very angry."*

HOMOPHOBIA

Homophobia is a dislike or fear of someone who is lesbian, gay or bisexual. At its mildest it is shown as resentment towards homosexuals but at its worst it is the cause of violent attacks.

FORMS OF HOMOPHOBIA

Homophobic behaviour can start very young when children use the word 'gay' as an insult, without even knowing the meaning of the word. This can build up to different types of homophobic bullying. The bully might spread rumours about someone's sexuality or behaviour by word of mouth, text messaging or computer chatrooms. Then there can be name-calling, socially isolating the victim, giving frightening looks, hitting and violent attacks.

As with any bullying, it causes misery to the person suffering the homophobia and often leads to levels of depression and other forms of mental ill-health. Bullying of any form is not acceptable.

> *"I contacted a youth worker who helped me set up a gay youth group and it grew and grew."*

Q What did you do?

It got to the point where I would break down, then I'd walk out of school and take myself to London. I sought out people openly gay to talk to. Then I started staying in London. I had very little money so I went to gay saunas or gay clubs and accepted offers, which gave me a bed for the night. Otherwise I slept rough.

Q Wasn't it risky for a teenage boy?

It was. When I slept on the streets there were people selling every kind of drug. People tried to rob you and there's always the chance of violence. Luckily I did know about safe sex so I protected myself in that way.

Q How did your parents react?

It was awful for them because they had no idea where I went or why I was rejecting them. But I had decided nobody understood me. When I was out of money and desperate I'd go home and then run away again. After two years of this they said that was enough. It was a shock to hear this and I realised how stupid I was being.

Q Did things improve?

Yes. Fortunately I got my GCSEs in spite of being out of school so much and I went to a sixth form where the guys were fine with me. I got involved with the local police diversity group and realised there was nothing for young gay people in the rural, conservative area where I lived. I contacted a youth worker who helped me set up a gay youth group and it grew and grew. But we had problems with people trying to break into our premises, a lot of name-calling and we needed police protection. Then I went to a gay youth

SECTION 28

Section 28 was the common name given to Section 2A of the Local Government Act of 1988. It forbade the promotion of homosexuality by local authorities and labelled gay family relationships as 'pretend'.

WHAT EFFECT DID IT HAVE IN SCHOOLS?

Many teachers felt that they were unable to include homosexuality when teaching sex education classes. It also made it difficult for them to help pupils who were suffering from homophobic bullying at school. It created a very confusing situation in schools and meant that many homosexuals felt they were not being treated fairly.

In reality, Section 28 never applied to individual schools. It was officially left to the head teachers to decide how they would teach sex education in their own schools.

REPEALING SECTION 28

In 2000, the government tried to get rid of Section 28. However, they faced great political opposition, particularly from the House of Lords who blocked its repeal.

Eventually, on September 18th 2003, the government repealed Section 28.

conference and heard about Stonewall, an organisation that campaigns on behalf of gays, and they were happy for me to do some volunteer work with them.

Q How valuable was that?

It made all the difference. I was with people who understood all I'd been through and I saw that I could help others in the same situation. My goal now is to set up a foundation for young gay and straight runaways to provide hostels where they can sleep, in every major city. At last, being gay is something I can be openly positive about. ■

LOSING MY RELATIONSHIP CONFIDENCE

Matt lost all his confidence after being rejected by his girlfriend. It took him some time before he moved on to a new relationship.

I met a girl who was a great personality and she seemed really into me. We started going out together. I had never had a long-term relationship and I was very besotted. At first she said she was, too.

Split personality

We moved in together and then she seemed to have two different personalities. When we were out she was really sociable, flirty and fun. But just with me she became reclusive. She flew off the handle a lot and I started to think there must be something wrong with me because she also blew hot and cold – passionate about me one minute, saying she didn't know why she was with me the next. I really wanted to be with her so I appeased her a lot.

Then she started going out on her own with girlfriends and she would have her phone off, and be out late. I discovered that she was sleeping with a guy I knew.

It hurt a lot but I so wanted to be with this girl that I tried to be understanding. Things went on like this for a year. I remember on her birthday I bought a machine to make bubbles and put party poppers on the door for when she came in. But she had been out the night before and she didn't come back.

Jealous

I became obsessively jealous about her and I felt terribly rejected believing I wasn't satisfying her as a lover. Then I came home one afternoon and found her in bed with someone else. I screamed at her it was the end and she moved out. I then found out she had been sleeping with lots of other people.

I was so unhappy, I kept crying myself to sleep. Having loved this girl so much really devastated me. My confidence went completely. I felt diminished.

Anxious

All this meant I was really anxious at the idea of starting a new relationship. I pushed away possibilities for a long time. Then I met someone else and we started up together but I don't think I was ready for another relationship although she made it plain she was mad about me. I think for me it was just being reassured that someone could really care for me. It didn't last. I was on my own for a while then but having a good, light-hearted time with women and making new friends. My confidence built up. During this time I met Jas and a friendship developed because we shared a lot of interests and we could talk about everything. I told her about the other girl and I was

able to see then that going through the rejection and the pain has made me emotionally stronger and with Jas I have got over the feeling of being sexually diminished. ∎

COPING WITH REJECTION

When you are dumped, it can leave you feeling crushed. If no reason is given for ending the relationship, bewilderment and pain can set in. It is easy to start blaming yourself for the break-up since no other explanation has been given.

LOSS OF CONFIDENCE

It is easy to lose confidence after a break-up. Try to be kind to yourself and stop looking for reasons why the relationship broke down. Focus on your positive points and in time your confidence will return.

NOT MEANT TO BE

Sometimes a relationship was not meant to be. Although it may have started well, feelings and circumstances can change.

Although it can be difficult to think of meeting new people when you are feeling low, it really helps to get out and be sociable. Pick up old hobbies and meet old friends as well as following new interests.

BECOMING A SINGLE PARENT

Juliet had an unplanned pregnancy as a teenager and would not advise others to become a parent so young.

Q How was your childhood?

I grew up on a farm run by a Camphill Rudolf Steiner community where my parents worked with people with special needs. There was a great sense that everyone cared about everyone else. It was a great place for a child.

Q When did you get pregnant?

I was about to do a degree in physical education. But before I began the course I found I was three and a half months pregnant by a man I had been seeing for about a

"I found I was three and a half months pregnant by a man I had been seeing for about a year."

TEENAGE PARENTS

Whatever your age, parenthood changes your life. Now you are responsible for the happiness, safety and health of someone else – and babies can be expensive. When parenthood happens to a teenager it can present challenges.

BECOMING A PARENT

When you become a parent there is a lot to learn. Your own parents, other young parents and health visitors can teach you what they know but some of it you have to pick up for yourself. It can build confidence to realise that you can cope with this baby and care for him/her but it is always good to seek help if you are struggling.

FEELING DIFFERENT

Being a teenage parent can make you feel different from your friends who are still free to please themselves, go out in the evening, follow career choices or go away to college. Making new friends with other young parents means you can talk about your baby and your life with people who are in a similar position.

MOVING ON

Just because you are a teenage parent doesn't mean you have to lose all your own dreams for the future. Seek advice on how to continue your education. You will be able to get help with the cost of childcare. Most colleges and universities and some work places have day nurseries where you can leave your baby or young child while you study or work. It might be more difficult to study or work but it isn't impossible.

year. I was 18 and he was seven years older. He wanted to get married and so we did before the baby was born. My parents were not happy about th way things happened but agreed that getting marrie was the right thing.

Q How did you feel about having a baby at this stage in your life?

I very young and was frightened at the prospect of becoming a mother. But my husband was there and Tamia's birth was a wonderful time. I felt, that night, that I loved my daughter more than anything in the world, and even though I was ill afterwards for six weeks and lost a lot of blood we bonded well.

Q Was your husband working to look after you and the baby?

He had a driving job and earned enough to support us. But he got a job which kept him out of t house from 6am until 10pm. When Tamia was a few months old I felt she needed her father more and he hardly seemed to be around. At this time my universi place which I had deferred came up. There was a loca crèche so I was very lucky. Tamia was six months and help me get around with her the Camphill communit bought me a car. I came back to see them and my parents fairly often because I valued the supportive environment there.

Q Were you and your husband getting on?

Through this first year I began to feel very disillusioned with my husband. I realised he would ▶

REVENTING
NWANTED
REGNANCIES

ou are sexually active you can obtain
traceptive advice from many places: your
surgery, a pharmacy, a family planning
ic or a walk-in centre. A professional
 advise you on the method that will suit
r lifestyle and health. There are many to
ose from.

NDOMS

doms are easy to obtain and prevent the
rm from reaching the egg. NHS clinics and
surgeries give them out free and they can
bought from chemists, supermarkets and
ding machines.

NTRACEPTIVE PILLS,
CHES AND INJECTIONS

se all work by changing the levels of
hormones in a woman's body to prevent
pregnancy. They are free with a
prescription.

DIAPHRAGMS AND CAPS

Like the condom, these prevent the sperm
from reaching the egg. The woman fits the
cap or diaphragm inside her vagina before
sex to provide a barrier against the sperm.

INTRAUTERINE DEVICE

This small device is placed inside the woman's
uterus to prevent pregnancy and stays there
for a period of time.

NATURAL FAMILY PLANNING

This is where a woman is taught how to
recognise changes in her body during the
menstrual cycle so that she knows when it is
safe to have sex. It requires training by a
health professional. It is less effective than
other methods.

EMERGENCY CONTRACEPTION

If you have had unprotected sex or your
usual contraceptive method has failed, act
quickly to obtain emergency contraception.
There are two methods: the emergency pill
can be bought from a pharmacist or
prescribed by your GP, or a temporary
intrauterine device (IUD) can be fitted.

er go anywhere with his work and had no
rest in making more of his life as I did. We rowed a
In December he went home to Zimbabwe. I chose
tay in London because I wanted to see how I
aged by myself. I managed tremendously and the
he came back I told him I was leaving. He was hurt
angry and I felt bad, but it was a bid for survival

Q So you preferred to be a single parent?

We were getting on so badly it seemed better. I found
somewhere to live for me and Tamia. My parents
showed their disappointment that my marriage hadn't
worked, and I didn't like that. We didn't speak for quite

> *"I wouldn't advise having a child so young. I have felt very trapped at times watching friends going travelling or having interesting social lives."*

Q What would you say to other young women?

I wouldn't advise having a child so young. I have felt very trapped at times watching friends going travelling or having interesting social lives. And I know it would have been a lot harder, and lonelier, without the huge support I have had from the Camphill community and my parents. But I love Tamia to bits and she has been a big incentive to make something of my life for her. ∎

a long time and I realised things were a good deal harder without the support of them and Camphill which had just been there before. But slowly the rift healed and then I went home in the holidays and spent time at Camphill.

Q Does Tamia see her father?

She sees a certain amount of him but it's been difficult because when he is angry with me he stops having anything to do with Tamia and that's hard for her. Sometimes I want to just put an end to the relationship altogether, but I know it's important for her to have a connection with her father, so I have to try to handle this.

Q Did you go on with university?

I went back to London for my second year and met a man doing law at my university. I used to help him study and I realised I could do the work and that inspired me to apply to Birmingham following my first degree with a two year degree for adults, in law. I split with the man and, as my parents' home is near Birmingham, I plan to live there while I study. Tamia can go to the Steiner school nearby and my mother will help.

YOUNG FATHER

Scott, 17, became a father soon after his 16th birthday. He very much wants to be a caring and supportive dad.

Q How old were you and Zosie when you got together?

We were at school together, but we got together as a couple just over a year ago. I was 16 and she was 13. We didn't see it as serious at first, but then our relationship developed and we had sex. We used contraceptives but not always. Sometimes we just didn't want to.

Q Did you consider sexually transmitted infections?

I don't really know about sexually transmitted infections, and anyway I don't think you get that if you go with someone you love.

Q Did you consider that Zosie might get pregnant?

I knew it was possible but I just didn't think it would happen to us. So when she phoned and told me I was very shocked and very angry. Angry at life, not at her. I threw my mobile phone across the room. I didn't want a baby so young. Zosie thought I wouldn't want anything to do with the baby and would run. She's seen boys my age doing that. ▶

"We used contraceptives but not always. Sometimes we just didn't want to."

COMMON MYTHS ABOUT SEX, PREVENTING PREGNANCY AND STIS

Everyone else is having sex.
False: Many people claim to be much more sexually active than is the case. The average age for a person to lose their virginity is 17.

I can't get pregnant if it is my first time.
False: You can get pregnant.

Once I've had unprotected sex I cannot protect myself from an unwanted pregnancy.
False: Emergency contraception can usually prevent pregnancy if taken within 72 hours.

If I use contraception, I cannot get pregnant.
False: No form of contraception is 100% effective. However, a family planning clinic can advise you on the best form of contraception for you.

I cannot get pregnant if I take a contraceptive pill.
False: If used correctly, the pill will give good protection against pregnancy but no contraception is 100% effective.

I can't get pregnant if my partner does not ejaculate.
False: Sperm can be released from the penis before ejaculation.

I can't get pregnant if I have my period.
False: It is possible to get pregnant all through the cycle.

I can catch a STI even though I've only ever slept with one person.
True: Although having fewer sexual partners cuts down your risk of catching a STI, you could still be infected.

I'll be able to tell if someone is carrying a STI as they will look ill.
False: Some people have no symptoms for years but they can still pass on a STI.

Oral sex is safe sex.
False: Although you cannot get pregnant from oral sex, you can catch certain STIs including herpes and Chlamydia.

THE RIGHTS OF THE TEENAGE DAD

Recently the law has changed to give more legal rights to teenage fathers. If the young man's name appears on his baby's birth certificate, this gives him shared parental rights. These rights include having a say in where the child will live, schooling, religion and health matters.

However, in practice it is up to the mother whether she allows the father's name to appear on the birth certificate. Without these legal rights, the teenage father has to go along with what the mother of the baby wants. A social worker may be able to help establish ways that the

Q Didn't you learn that from your parents?

My dad left my mum when she was pregnant and my mum never coped with me and my three half-brothers. Age seven I was taken into care. I had a rubbish childhood. I was moved 15 times. The foster parents all said they couldn't cope with me because I was very difficult and abusive. I didn't feel anyone wanted me until the last family where I was for four years. But I've moved out now. They aren't interested in being involved with me and my baby.

Q Are you living with Zosie and Ben?

I'm not allowed to because Zosie is too young. Because I've left care my social worker Bea has organised for me to live in a half-way house run by Pam Bihar. I see Zosie and Ben most days. She is living with her mum so I go over there. I do everything with the baby. I change nappies, I feed him, I take him for walks.

Q And did you think of leaving Zosie and having nothing to do with the baby?

I very soon got used to the idea and I began to feel pleased. I told Zosie I would be there as a parent. And I was with her when she gave birth to Ben. That was amazing – really thrilling. But what made it difficult was never having seen adults being parents.

Q So do you feel Zosie's mum is supporting both of you?

I do, but she quite often kicks me out if I am arguing a lot with Zosie. Pam tells me to watch my behaviour and not let myself get at Zosie. I don't much like that, but I do know she is trying to help me keep contact with Ben. She says I have been better since Ben was born. It frightens me that Ben's social worker might decide I'm not good for him because of my fights with Zosie.

"I do everything with the baby. I change nappies, I feed him, I take him for walks."

> "I want to be able to support him and Zosie so I need to find work."

Q Do you think about the future?

We have friends with a child a bit older so we see what each stage means. I know I will have to take Ben to playschool and then to big school. But I want to be able to support him and Zosie so I need to find work. I would like to be a lorry driver but I can't do that until I'm 21 and I don't know what I want to do before that. I see a Connexions worker each week to discuss how I might get work.

Q Is Zosie happy with the situation?

Zosie says she thinks it's all right being such young parents but I don't know how it would be if we lived together alone. I know I haven't got a grip on my emotions well enough and when Pam told me the other day that the baby's feelings have to come first I found myself just saying, 'Nobody put my feelings first'. I think that still makes me upset.

Q So do you think about the future?

I love to imagine us all in a house as a family one day. I have to prove to Zosie I am serious about being a father. Well I am. I feel very close to Ben. He is the first thing I have really done right and I care about him a lot. ∎

CHILDHOOD ABUSE

The abuse Ami suffered throughout childhood at the hands of her stepfather led to depression and difficulty making relationships. But she feels life is improving now.

Q How was your childhood?

My mum and dad split when I was four. My younger brother and I lived alone with Mum then she met my stepdad. At first he was really nice, playing with us a lot. And Mum seemed happier. My stepdad moved in when I was six.

Q When did his behaviour become inappropriate?

I think it was inappropriate before he moved in; it made me uneasy but I just assumed it was normal. Before he moved in Mum would drop us round for babysitting and he would touch me intimately and show me bits of his body. I wanted to tell Mum but he said it would make her unhappy and that would be my fault. He also said he'd hurt me if I told Mum. Then on my eighth birthday he kept saying, 'I've got a really special birthday present for you.' Of course I was excited and he said I could have it later, when Mum went out.

> *"I remember telling him to stop, that it was hurting and he told me to be quiet because I'd wake my brother."*

Q Were you happy about that?

Not really because I knew what normally happened when she went out to work in the evenings. I was watching TV in my room and my stepdad came in. He said it's time for your birthday present. Then he raped me. I remember telling him to stop, that it was hurting and he told me to be quiet because I'd wake my brother. So I lay there and when he'd finished he said, 'Happy birthday'. That was the beginning and it happened all the time Mum was out until I left home aged 19. I tried to stop him once and he hit me really hard, but where it wouldn't show. ▶

CHILD ABUSE

While most children and young people receive the love and care they need, some are abused by their parents or other adults. This abuse can take different forms. Whatever form it takes, child abuse is always wrong. If it is happening to you tell another adult, for example at school, or contact one of the organisations on page 31.

SEXUAL ABUSE
Sometimes an adult forces or persuades a child or young person to join in sexual acts. This might involve being kissed, touched sexually, looking at pornography or being forced to have sex. It can occur with an adult or in a group.

PHYSICAL ABUSE
This is when a child or young adult is hit, shaken, kicked or violently attacked by parents or adults. All these acts will result in pain and can cause serious injury.

EMOTIONAL ABUSE
Some adults criticise, treat harshly and reject their own children, or children in their care. They show little affection or interest in them.

NEGLECT
When a child or young person does not receive enough food, good clothing, love and attention from parents or other adult carers this is called neglect. It is a form of child abuse as it means the child is suffering hunger, cold, poor health and lack of mental well-being.

OVERCOMING CHILD ABUSE
Child abuse can be very damaging to the person who is abused. When they grow up they can struggle to come to terms with what happened to them. It can cause many problems including depression, low self-esteem and problems with relationships. Counsellors, social workers and the NSPCC (National Society for the Prevention of Cruelty to Children) offer help and support.

How did it make you feel?

I thought there must be something wrong with me because he kept hurting me and he said I was bad. I couldn't tell Mum I was doing these things with her husband and he put me on the pill so I didn't get pregnant. I cut my feelings off as hard as I could. When I reached my teens I stopped eating. I couldn't control what he was doing, but I could take control over my body that way. And although I had been close to my mother before my stepdad moved in, she seemed to have little time for me and was preoccupied with him. I lost a lot of weight and started cutting my arms and legs.

Did your mother see how unhappy you were then?

No. In school a few teachers noticed I had lost weight but I just said I was okay. One teacher saw bruises on me and social services visited home but my parents convinced them all was fine. I was desperate and hated myself. When I was 17 my real dad who I had met and hoped to move in with killed himself. I took an overdose and ended up in a psychiatric unit. When I left I was given cognitive behavioural therapy which was helpful, and I started writing poems which has been valuable.

> *"I was desperate and hated myself."*

Q Did you have relationships?

I had a boyfriend but I couldn't sleep with him for ages. When I tried it felt bad and wrong so I ended the relationship. At 19 I got a job in a bar and left home but I was very disconnected, just existing for several years. I met the odd man but the moment I felt happy I panicked and broke it off. Then I met the dad of my baby and sex was good most of the time. I didn't tell him what had happened but I felt I had managed to create a strong relationship at last.

Q So was the pregnancy planned?

I wanted it but he decided to leave when I was halfway through the pregnancy, so I have been on my own with my son Ethan. That's made me realise I have to get on with life and be a grown-up because he is worth doing it for; he's the one person I can really love. My relationship with my mother is pretty well non-existent and I don't want her around Ethan when she is drunk. Otherwise I might have gone home because my stepdad died.

Q Was that liberating?

No. I just felt he had got away with everything. He wrecked my life and the scars are still there but I'll never have the chance to make him suffer. I just wish I had dared to speak out when it first happened. ■

GLOSSARY

androgynous
A blending of male and female attitudes, roles, looks or characteristics.

bisexual
A person who is emotionally and/or sexually oriented towards both sexes.

condom
A tube of very thin rubber, which is closed at one end, that a man puts over his penis before sexual intercourse. It is used as a contraceptive and also to stop sexual infections. See page 20.

contraceptive
Something that stops a woman getting pregnant. The most popular methods are the pill and condoms (see page 20), but other methods such as injectable contraception are available. Doctors and local family planning centres give advice as to which form of contraception is best for each person.

emergency contraception
An emergency method to prevent pregnancy. There are two types of emergency contraception – pills and IUDs. Pills can be taken up to 72 hours from the time of unprotected sex. An IUD can be inserted up to 96 hours or four days after unprotected sex. Emergency contraception is not a form of abortion because it prevents a pregnancy occurring. The sooner it is used the more effective it is.

family planning
A general term to describe deciding how many children you want to have. Also refers to the methods you can use which are also called contraception and birth control.

heterosexual
A person whose sexual attraction and desire is for people of the opposite sex.

homophobia
Homophobia is the fear, dislike of or discrimination against homosexuality or homosexuals. It can also mean hatred, hostility, or disapproval of homosexual people, sexual behaviour, or cultures.

homosexuality
Being sexually attracted to people of the same sex.

one-night stand
A single sexual encounter between two people, where at least one of them is not intending to or expecting to have a longer-term sexual or romantic relationship.

pill
A form of contraceptive, taken by a woman. See page 20.

porn
Short for pornography – writing, pictures or films that have been created to stimulate sexual desire.

rape
To force someone to have sex against their will.

safe sex
Ways in which people reduce the risk of getting sexually transmitted infections, for example by using condoms.

sexually transmitted infection (STI)
Infections such as HIV, Chlamydia and gonorrhoea, amongst others. Most STIs can be easily diagnosed and treated, but some have serious consequences. The best way to avoid them is to use condoms during sexual intercourse.

virginity
Virginity is the state of never having had sexual intercourse.

FURTHER INFORMATION

British Pregnancy Advisory Service
Actionline: 08457 30 40 30
Web: www.bpas.org
The *leading provider of abortion services in the UK.*

Brook
Free helpline: 0800 0185 023
Web: www.brook.org.uk
Provides youth advisory and birth control clinics for young people. Gives sexual advice, carries out pregnancy tests and offers help and support for unplanned and unwanted pregnancy.

Careline
Tel: 0845 122 8622
Web: www.carelineuk.org
Telephone counselling for people of any age, on any issue.

Get Connected
Free helpline: 0808 808 4994
Web: www.getconnected.org.uk
Helpline for young people.

Marie Stopes
Tel: 0845 300 8090
Web: www.mariestopes.org.uk
A health organisation that works to prevent unintended pregnancies and unwanted births by offering advice, contraceptive services and abortions.

One Parent Families/Gingerbread
Web: www.oneparentfamilies.org.uk
Lone Parent Helpline: 0800 018 5026
Offers information and advice to lone parents.

Samaritans
Tel: 08457 90 90 90
Web: www.samaritans.org.uk
Support for anyone in crisis.

Sexwise
Free advice line: 0800 28 29 30
Web: www.ruthinking.co.uk
Offers free, confidential advice on sex, relationships and contraception.

Single parent action network
Web: www.singleparents.org.uk
An organisation set up to create a voice for single parents and their children and to empower families.

Stonewall
Tel: 020 7593 1850
www.stonewall.org.uk
Stonewall works for equality and justice for lesbians, gay men and bisexuals and runs campaigns to tackle homophobia and homophobic bullying.

There4me
Web: www.there4me.com
Email support service for young people between 12-16 years.

Youth Access
Helpline: 020 8896 3675
Web: www.youthaccess.org.uk
Counselling services for young people aged 12–25 years.

Youth2Youth
Web: www.youth2youth.co.uk
Email and telephone support, run by young volunteers for under 19s.

www.teenissues.co.uk
Articles with information and advice on the perils and issues that plague teens.

www.thesite.org
Articles on young people's issues including health and wellbeing.

www.queeryouth.org.uk
A website for gay and transgendered young people.

www.young-voice.org
A charity that researches views of young people. It has a database of 7,000 young people's views on different issues.

www.positive.org
The website of the Coalition for Positive Sexuality (CPS) which gives information for teens on how to take care of themselves and in so doing affirm their decisions about sex, sexuality and reproductive control.

www.kidshelp.com.au
Free helpline: 1800 55 1800

Telephone and online counselling for young people under 25.

www.youthline.co.nz

Support for young people in New Zealand.

INDEX

TALKING POINTS

The interviews in this book may provoke a range of reactions: shock, surprise, empathy. As many of the interviewees found, talking can help you to sort out your emotions. If you wish to talk about the interviews here are some questions to get you started:

Janine's story - page 6

How far do you agree that women's magazines promote sleeping around? Why do you think someone with low self-esteem is more likely to take risks?

James' story - page 8

What do you think of James' attitude towards the women he sleeps with? Is he behaving acceptably? What do you think of his statement that he doesn't respect girls who sleep around?

Shari's story - page 10

How important do you think the Internet is for young gay people?

Joe's story - page 12

What could Joe's school have done to help him when he

started to suffer from bullying? What do you think schools should teach about gay sexuality?

Matt's story - page 16

Why do you think Matt's confidence was so badly knocked? What ways can you think of to get over a failed relationship?

Juliet's story - page 18

Juliet's parents thought that getting married was the right thing to do for the baby. Do you agree that the parents of a child should be married?

Scott's story - page 22

Scott didn't know much about STIs, or indeed contraception. What do you think is the best way to educate young people about sex and contraception? Why do you think there are so many myths surrounding sex?

Ami's story - page 26

Why do you think it was difficult to tell her mother or another adult about what was happening to her? What are the difficulties for social services in dealing with this kind of case?

These are the lists of contents for each title in *Talking About Myself*:

Depression
What is depression? • All alone • Love's lost • Drug-taking depression • Accepting the past • Years of depression • Managing meltdown - bipolar disorder • Pushy parent • Attempted suicide

Eating Disorders
What are eating disorders? • Recovering anorexic • Fighting bulimia • Reaction to bullying - male anorexia • Dangerous images • Symptom of depression • From obese to bulimic • Fighting obesity • Feeling good at last

Losing a loved one
Coping with loss • Living with guilt • Losing a brother • Keeping a friend in mind • Caring for my mother • Holding on to memories - losing a granddad • Coping with a tragic death • Hearing from abroad • Feeling betrayed

My family
What is a family? • Dealing with divorce • When my parents split up • Father and son difficulties • Keeping the peace • Difficult at any age • Meeting my father for the first time • Care and adoption • Caring for my mother

Racism
What is racism? • Trying to belong - a Muslim's story • Culture clash • Being the outsider • Anti-Semitic attack • Bullied by other Muslims • Breaking down racism • Not allowed to mix • Growing up with racism

Relationships & Sex
First relationhips • Sleeping around • Sex without attachment • Glad to be gay • Dealing with homophobia • Losing my relationships confidence • Becoming a single parent • Young father • Childhood abuse